Achieve Your Dreams

Written and compiled by Kathleen Russell and Larry Wall

Published by
Walrus Productions

Published by Walrus Productions
4805 NE 106th St, Seattle, Washington, 98125.

Text layout typography by Steve Norman of The Durland Group

Printed by Vaughan Printing, Nashville, Tennessee

Russell, Kathleen F.
    Achieve Your Dreams / [compiled and arranged by]
Kathleen F. Russell, Larry C. Wall.
        p. cm.
        ISBN   09635176-3-5

    1. Quotations. 2. American wit and humor.   I. Wall, Larry C.   II. Title.

PN6084.H8R87 1994   808.8'2
                                      QBI94-1015

Printed in the United States of America
10 9 8 7 6 5 4 3

INTRODUCTION

We have assembled this unique collection of whimsical words of wisdom in the hope that others will share the inspiration, humor and reflections they have given to us.

ACKNOWLEDGMENTS

We deeply appreciate the contributions from those people that helped guide and motivate us in producing this book:

Bryan Stringer, Teri Gillet, Cathy Burr, Dorothy Wall, Ronald Russell, Mark Gilman, Bruce Ungari, Jim Anderson, Don McCann, Dave Orsinger, Don Jordan, Maureen Kerschbaum, Pete Maher, Deanna Potts, Steve & Margie Norman, Bob Baum, Sandy Morse, Mike Roberts, Bill Parranto, Frank Cloak, John Crum, Jimmy Bloom, Dick Nickoloff, Gayle Goldman, Mary Lee Muslin, Barbara Blais, Sandy Ussery, Kit Corson, Sel Polsky, Diane Pringle, Bob Alling, Rodney Moyer, Paul Gaudette, Barry Lacasse, Joanne White, Ed Delfin, Jan Savage Warner, Louis Seaman, Dan Mealey, Tim Fedora, Bob Jordan, Ronald Winter, Michael Short, Patty Portman, Dave Rinaldo, Eve Meridith, Stan Arnold, Jack McElgunn, Bonnie Hunt, John Derrick, Bill Asaff, Henry Levy, Cy Greenbaum, Jay Picciolo, Damian Abernathy, Barbara Quammen, Julie Scesniak, Gene Faulkenberry, Coleman Farr, Steve Sams, Michelle Canterbury, Georgia Reagan, Janet Stein, Bruce Muller, John Donham, Marcy Johnson, Jonathan Hatfield, Ronnie Lavin, Barb Frank, Kent Osterman, Brett Birdsong, Barb Mathiasen, Len Parranto, Richard Kratner, Carol Wade, Bill Hall Pat Maliha, Karen Tatman, Michael Manelis, Joan & Rennee Roux, Erin Angel, Louis Faber, Lisa Rudley, Sandra Yaros, Carolyn Allen , Dorothy Jenner, Nancy Deigan, Betsy Northrop, Larry & Janet McEwin, Sherry Davis, Mary Steinkamp, Barbara Kramr, Jim Burleson, Sharon Ellsberry, Darlene Mills, Mark Alton, Carolyn Sery, Carolyn Smolich, Stephanie Chupein, Susan Douglas, Diane Girard, Mary Jane Spagnolo, Thor Anderson, Paul Borne, Jeffery Sugarman, Cindy Zaring, Dave January, Steve Griffin, David Kaplowitz, Ric & Carol Samuels, Chryssa MacCutcheon, Peggy Hanson, Marie Stewart, Cheryl Anderson, Art Cikins, Robert Epstein, Colette Leonard, Lise McManus, Ben Van Dow, Annette & Nancy Cogan, Scott Moskovitz, Billy Woodard & Vaughan Printing.

Life is what happens while you are making other plans.

The key to happiness and success is to have a dream.

You have to wake up,
in order for your dreams
to come true.

Greet the dawn
with enthusiasm
and you may expect
satisfaction at sunset.

If you want the rainbow you gotta put up with the rain.

Don't prepare for rainy days without enjoying today's sunshine.

Stand for something
or you'll fall for anything.

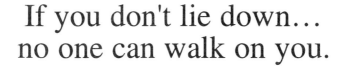

If you don't lie down…
no one can walk on you.

Motivation is when your dreams put on work clothes.

You are never
fully dressed until
you wear a smile.

Happiness is the journey…
not the destination.

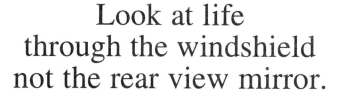

Look at life
through the windshield
not the rear view mirror.

A man without humor is like a car without shock absorbers.

A fancy car
is not the key to success,
it's the driver.

Make sure your world
isn't filled with
one-way, dead end streets.

Experience
is the one thing
you can't get
on *easy payments*.

All play and no work does not work.

Some people dream of
worthy accomplishments,
while others stay awake
and achieve them.

You are not late
until you get there.

Give your troubles to God,
He will be up all night
anyway.

Do it now!
You become successful
the moment you start.

Each of us has two ends,
a sitting end
and a thinking end.
Success depends
on which we use.

Remember,
no one can make
you feel inferior
without your consent.

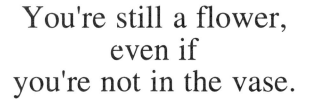

You're still a flower,
even if
you're not in the vase.

Bloom where you're planted.
All the flowers of tomorrow
are in the seeds of today.

A person of words
and not deeds
is like a garden
full of weeds.

Happiness *held*
is the seed.
Happiness *shared*
is the flower.

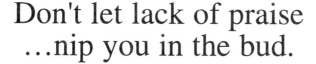

Don't let lack of praise
...nip you in the bud.

Count your age
by friends.
Count your life
by smiles.

Smile!
It increases
your face value.

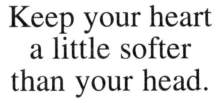

Keep your heart
a little softer
than your head.

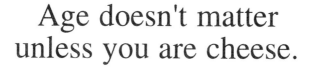

Age doesn't matter
unless you are cheese.

Growing old is when fun is a lot more work.

If you think things
improve with age,
attend a class reunion.

God gave us two ears
and one mouth.
Think twice, speak once!

The words you speak today
should be soft and tender…
for tomorrow
you may have to eat them.

Advice would be more
acceptable
if it didn't always
conflict with our plans.

It's what you learn
after you know it all
that counts.

A goal is a dream
with a deadline.

People with goals succeed
because they know
where they are going.

You can not discover
new oceans unless
you have the courage
to lose sight of the shore.

To succeed,
do the best you can,
where you are,
with what you have.

Don't wait for your ship to come in… swim out to it.

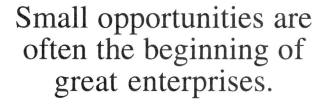

Small opportunities are
often the beginning of
great enterprises.

Remember, there's
nothing more constant
than change.

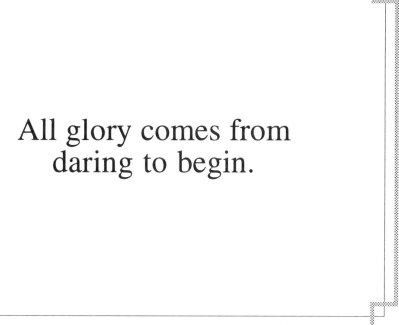

All glory comes from daring to begin.

Remember change
and change for the better
are two different things.

The only place success
comes before work
is in the dictionary.

The greater part of progress is the desire to progress.

The trouble with using
experience as a guide,
is that the final exam
often comes first...
then comes the lesson.

Destiny…
is not a matter of chance
it's a matter of choice.

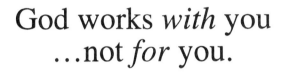

God works *with* you
…not *for* you.

Temptation comes easy, opportunity takes longer.

Happiness is a choice …not a response.

If you are
not having problems,
you are missing
an opportunity for growth.

To achieve your dreams
believe in yourself.
If you don't, who will?

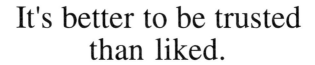

It's better to be trusted than liked.

Underpromise
Overperform.

Measure twice, cut once.

People forget how fast
you did a job,
but they will remember
how well you did it.

To hurry is like burning down your own house …to get rid of a rat.

It doesn't pay
to be in a hurry.
You pass up much more
than you catch up with.

You always pass failure on the way to success.

Be glad you didn't get
everything you thought
you wanted, when you
thought you wanted it.

If at first
you don't succeed,
try, try again. Then quit.
There's no use in being
a fool about it.

Life's real failure is
when you do not realize
how close you were
to success
when you gave up.

The surest way to go broke
is to sit around
and wait for a break.

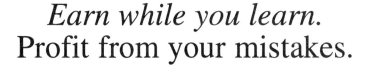

Earn while you learn.
Profit from your mistakes.

The best way
to predict the future
...is to invent it.

The difference between
ordinary & extraordinary
is just that little *extra*.

A natural tendency is
to want to be understood
rather than understand.

We can be knowledgeable
with other men's knowledge,
but we can't be wise
with other men's wisdom.

It takes a smart man
to know he's not.

Life must be lived forwards but can only be understood backwards.

Don't waste fresh tears
over old griefs. You may
need those tears tomorrow.

Nothing lasts forever except a bad movie.

Don't think there are
no crocodiles
just because
the water is calm.

Never insult a crocodile
until you've
crossed the river.

A good scare
is sometimes
worth more to a man
than good advice.

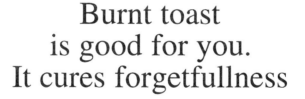

Burnt toast
is good for you.
It cures forgetfullness

Some men
make difficulties.
Difficulties
make some men.

A candle loses
none of its light by
lighting another candle.

Experience
is the best teacher
because it's
always on the job.

A new broom sweeps clean,
but the old brush
knows the corners.

The greatest mistake
you can make is to
be afraid of making one.

If your dreams
turn to dust
…vacuum.

Today is the tomorrow
you worried about yesterday,
but not enough.

If you've seen yesterday
and you love today,
you won't be afraid of
tomorrow.

The reward of
of a job well done
is being the one who did it.

Never notice
what *has* to be done.
See only…
what *remains* to be done.

No one fails
who does his best.
No one succeeds
at home at rest.

Does your employer
consider you profit
...or overhead?

Spend as much time
providing customer service
as you do talking about it.

Short answers
save trouble.
The shortest answer
is to do it.

Many of us spend
half our time wishing
for things we could have
if we didn't spend half
our time wishing.

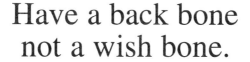

Have a back bone
not a wish bone.

If you have a job
without aggravation,
you don't really
have a job.

Don't let your
voice mail be
"voice jail"
to your callers.

The mind is
not a warehouse
to be needlessly filled,
but an instrument
to be used resourcefully.

Many people quit
looking for work…
when they finally
get a job.

Every job
is a self portrait
of those who did it.

Autograph your work with quality.

Pursue one great decisive aim with force and with determination.

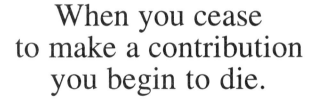

When you cease
to make a contribution
you begin to die.

If you tell the truth,
sooner or later
somebody's going to
find you out.

Be on the level
and you won't
go downhill.

A liar needs
a good memory.
There's nothing so pathetic
as a forgetful liar.

You can be happy without
expecting others to
agree with you.

Happiness is the place between too little and too much.

The time to relax
is when
you don't have time for it.

Love at first sight
is no miracle.
When two people have been
looking at each other for years
that's a miracle.

Love at first sight
saves a lot of time.

Those who hug
illusions seldom
embrace opportunity.

Wisdom
is what's left over
after we smarten up.

We can't spell
S CCESS
without U.

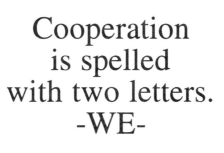

Cooperation
is spelled
with two letters.
-WE-

Get your facts first,
then you can distort them
as much as you please.

If you can't get people
to listen to you,
tell them…
it's confidential.

Time flies like arrows.
Fruit flies like bananas.

If it wasn't for the last minute… nothing would get done.

About the only thing
that comes
to us without effort
is old age.

Your children
need your presence
more than your presents.

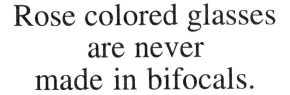

Rose colored glasses
are never
made in bifocals.

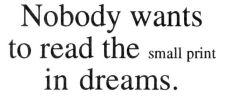

Nobody wants
to read the small print
in dreams.

The only thing worse than an alarm going off is one that doesn't.

The best way
out of difficulty
…is through it.

For every person who
climbs the ladder of success,
there are a dozen
waiting for the elevator.

Ladder of Achievement

100%	I did
90%	I will
80%	I can
70%	I think I can
60%	I might
50%	I think I might
40%	What is it?
30%	I wish I could
20%	I don't know how
10%	I can't
0%	I won't

People may doubt
what you say
but they will believe
what you do.

A great pleasure in life
is doing what people
say cannot be done.

In the end,
the only people
who fail are those
who do not try.

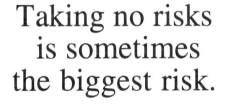

Taking no risks
is sometimes
the biggest risk.

Everything has been
thought of before,
the challenge
is to think of it again.

Some people succeed
because they're destined to.
Most succeed because they
are *determined* to.

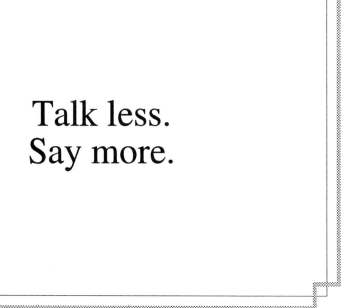

Talk less.
Say more.

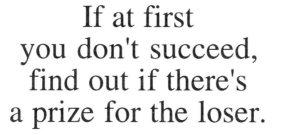

If at first
you don't succeed,
find out if there's
a prize for the loser.

You can only
control two things
…your attitude
and your activity.

Never forget the kindergarten principle: Keep it fun.

A mistake is a lesson
on its way
to be learned.

Don't give failure
a bad name.

The only sure
thing about luck:
it will change.

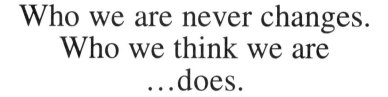

Who we are never changes.
Who we think we are
...does.

Persistence may be
the key to success,
but the key to failure
...is trying to
please everybody.

Success...
Don't do what you like,
like what you do.

Any concern too small
to be made into a prayer,
is too small to be made
into a burden.

Thankfulness can turn
an ordinary tune,
…into a concert.

To forgive but
not forget is like
burying the hatchet with
the handle sticking out.

Be careful about reading
health books…
you may die of a misprint.

To worry is like
wondering what wine
goes with fingernails.

If you think nobody
cares you're alive,
try missing a few
car payments.

The reverse side also has a reverse side.

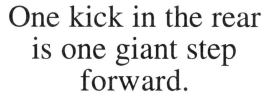

One kick in the rear
is one giant step
forward.

To be is to do. (Socrates)
To do is to be. (Plato)
Do be do be do. (Sinatra)

He who laughs last might have needed it explained.

May each day's thought give wings to your work and your dreams.